Plant Your Garden In A Keyhole

W. LEON SMITH

Smith Media, Inc. Books

SᴹIᴵB

Smith Media, Inc. Books

Published by Smith Media, Inc.
1503 W. 11th St., Clifton, TX 76634
books@smithmediainc.com.

First Edition

ISBN: 978-0-9969006-1-4

Library of Congress Control Number: 2015918480

Published by Smith Media, Inc.

Printed in the United States of America

DEDICATION

This book is dedicated to my grandparents, Jim and Gladys Smith
and Charlie and Alicia Lovell, all avid gardeners and farmers
during the golden days of yesteryear, notably in the early 20th century.

CONTENTS

PREFACE

Keyhole gardening in America is coming of age as more and more gardeners learn of its existence and of the many benefits that this type of raised-bed system provides.

Plant Your Garden In A Keyhole presents a general overview of this without going into many of the deeper scientific aspects. The book is based on my experiences during several years of experimenting with and raising successful crops in keyhole gardens.

I hope readers find the book helpful in making a decision about trying this type of gardening. Personally, I would never go back to traditional on-the-ground row gardening and am continuously amazed at how my keyhole gardens produce.

A few years ago my brother and I developed an easy-to-put-together keyhole garden kit under the name Keyhole Farm, LLC. On its website, www.keyholefarm.com, are numerous photographs depicting crops we have raised at our experiment station. Also included are some how-to methods we have developed.

One of the aspects of keyhole gardening that I feel is important is the use of its wire internal basket, sometimes referred to as a tube or cylinder, for recycling table scraps. Not only does this basket provide quite a bit of moisture for the plants grown adjacent to it in the main bed, but as the basket contents decompose, natural nutrients are disbursed in the main garden, thereby limiting and usually eliminating the need for commercial fertilizers.

Too, it is my belief that teaching youngsters about gardening will add a whole new dimension to their lives – one that extends to an appreciation and more thorough understanding of Mother Nature while providing them with a true-life adventure as they raise their own crops.

With a quickly changing world, the future lies in the ability to raise quality crops. What better way to do this than with your own backyard mini-farm where plants are compacted into a raised-bed garden that conserves water, where a lot of backbreaking work associated with traditional gardens is eliminated, and where you control your own soil that is accentuated with recycling?

Not only does keyhole gardening provide fresh, delicious, healthy food for your dinner table, it is also a fabulous means of escape as you step into the universe of plants and learn more about the way Mother Nature organizes her life-sustaining harvests.

Before: Girl Scouts plant seeds...

Afterward: An overflowing harvest!

planted a traditional garden (see photos), complete with a scarecrow, and raised some admirable crops.

However, there was a downside.

CHAPTER ONE
My Entry Into
Keyhole Gardening

Although the concept of keyhole gardening has been around for several years since its origination at a school in Lesotho, Africa, many gardeners are yet to realize that this near-perfect gardening system is revolutionary when it comes to raising crops while recycling in the process.

I have been around gardens all my life, from the time my mom raised one in Hamilton, Texas when I was a kid, to neighbors who had a garden and allowed me to stomp on dirt clods where potatoes were to be planted, to my grandmother's garden, where I enjoyed attacking grasshoppers on hot summer days.

A few years ago my wife and I

Gardening can be backbreaking work, dealing with weeds, bending down to pick veggies almost daily, and digging the rows and planting them. Then there is the constant chore of moving the water hoses and sprinklers. Unfortunately, a lot of the watering only serves to give thirsty weeds a drink, and it doesn't take much for them to get their fill and grow very fast and very big.

Ultimately, we gave up gardening after a few years. The amount of time it took pulling weeds was almost as cumbersome as the labor associated with the chore itself — it was very hard on the back. We did not want to inject dangerous chemicals into the soil, so we called it quits. Afterward, my wife continued to raise tomatoes in flower beds, but that was about it. I missed my very tasty home-grown watermelons and the masses of green beans and black-eyed peas that we had produced in the vacant lot that was our garden.

In January of 2009 I needed to get rid of some rocks that had been piled next to the walls at the back of my business. They had sat there for about eight years, in the way, after I had removed them to open a doorway to allow access to two structures. They had been part of an internal rock wall. I published a weekly newspaper there that had recently featured a column by Dr. Deb Tolman, who holds a doctorate in environmental sciences and geography from Portland State University, about the virtues of a relatively new concept – keyhole gardening. Dr. Tolman, a genius when it comes to gardening concepts, especially keyholes, provided the how-to and the expected returns. This made me again wish that I still had a garden.

Since the rocks behind the business simply had to go, I put two and two together and decided to haul the rocks

to a house on my residential property and build such a garden. "Dr. Deb's" newspaper article was so convincing that I thought, "Why not build one?"

After a lot of consideration as to the perfect location for the new keyhole garden, I decided to locate the garden near a sidewalk behind my storage house. It was here that a friend and I dumped the rocks after hauling them there in the back of a pickup. Moving the rocks was a pain — a royal pain, which made me question if this was actually a good idea.

I carefully prepared the measurements that I was going to use in structuring the garden and got busy laying out the rocks; they were HEAVY.

I stacked them to form the circular shape so that there wasn't much gap in the placements.

The rocks were in a variety of shapes and sizes, so it was akin to putting a jigsaw puzzle together to get the best fit. None of the pieces fit perfectly; there were holes to deal with.

Then I had a major problem. Not enough rocks. So, to improvise, I used cinder blocks for the second half of the structure, sort of. After positioning the "cinder/rocks" into the six-foot diameter design, I got a bag of concrete and filled the holes, trying to make the structure sturdier, which worked. Patching the holes was more labor intensive than I had counted on, but I gradually got it done.

The design was approximately three feet high. I used cinder blocks to frame the wedge to be cut out of the circle

and designed a cage for the internal basket out of two types of fencing that I had lying about. Most of it was chicken wire. It is in this interior circle where I would "feed" the garden with scraps, etc. and it is where a lot of the watering took place.

Next, to begin filling the garden, I tried to layer the bottom parts of the main section with wetted-down cardboard straight out of a wheelbarrow where I had dumped water to near capacity. I also layered the bed with small tree limbs, brown leaves, grass clippings, compost, green leaves, coffee grounds, and dirt. I had cut some plastic trash bags to put around the interior edges of the garden in the event I did not get all the holes patched well enough, just in case. I didn't want the dirt to leak out when it rained.

Eventually I was nearing the top where I dumped quite a few bags of clean topsoil to build the shape I wanted.

Next came planting — rather, deciding what to plant. I figured that this first year's garden would be primarily experimental, so I bought several packets of seeds locally and a few packets I ordered online (long-term heirloom garden type brands). Some I knew would probably not produce crops down in Texas, since they are designed for "northern" climates, but I thought I would give them a try.

Here is a diagram that shows my

3

planting scheme.

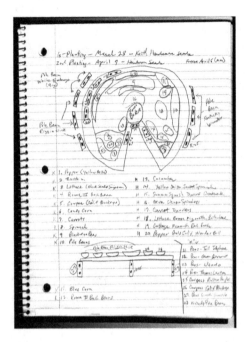

Just as the initial plants barely cleared the dirt the region had a freeze in early April. I had covered the top (very carefully) with taped-together newsprint to maybe help a little the night before when I became aware of the impending freeze, but I lost several green bean plants. They slowly turned yellow and died. Some of the other plants might have been impacted, as well, but I am not absolutely sure. However, I did the planting in two waves, the first on March 28 and the second on April 7. It was part of my plan to stagger their placement into the soil. The freeze happened on April 6.

I also erected panels of wire fencing on two sides of the garden in the event vines wanted to climb up them. Several

did.

I spent about 10-15 minutes a day watering from a hose and sprinkler attachment, unless it rained. There's no use washing your car in a rainstorm, so I figured that applied to plants as well. However, I did miss watering on a few sunny days when I felt the garden was moist enough.

My first plants to come up and bear fruit were yellow crook-neck squash and green zucchini. In fact, their leaves really overtook the garden, so much that there were times I didn't know there was something ready to be picked. They were hiding. My carrots, bell peppers, and lettuce did fairly well, but the shade from the other plants taught me to locate them better for more production.

neglected the garden as a result. I did pull up the black-eyes when their production declined, but did nothing to the giant okra pods, now dead on the vine.

I planted several types of black-eyed peas. Some were purple, some green, and some were called cowpeas. By summertime, they were producing like crazy. Every other day I would pick a mess big enough for a meal and, if picked correctly, a new pod would start growing in its place. This went on for about two months, maybe a little longer. Mid-summer, I pulled up the squash and zucchini and planted okra.

These grew into very tall plants and produced in abundance. Their pods have to be watched closely since they get big almost overnight. Too big and they are too hard to properly cook (I was lectured on this when I brought in some gigantic pods). But I was flabbergasted at how much - they produced.

During the spring growing season the area experienced a lot of rain early-on (like May), but it got very dry in the middle of the summer (up to 104 degrees F).

Toward the end of the summer growing season I got busy with several time-consuming business concerns (not related to keyhole gardening) and

The garden lay dormant in the late fall and winter as I contemplated round two and anticipated the coming spring.

During late winter, I pulled up any remaining dead plants and found I needed to repack the main content since the soil had sunken about eight inches. When I dug around in the soil, I realized that the contents of the lower layers had mostly decomposed and the soil was dark and rich.

To refill the main content, I would dig a wide hole in an area about three-quarters down, piling the dirt in an adjoining area. In the hole I placed fresh clippings, leaves, green material, newsprint, and cardboard, along with the okra stalks that I had recently pulled up, and then covered it up with the dirt I had shifted to the side. I went around the whole garden doing this, which was really fairly easy since the digging of loose dirt took little effort.

Then, to complete the fill, I added some fresh topsoil/compost mix on the surface, stirred it with some of the original soil below, and replanted.

In a blog, I wrote, "It is somewhat exciting to get back in the groove on my keyhole garden and try to learn from mistakes made last year. I do know for sure I'll grow black-eyed peas, squash, and zucchini, and probably a bunch of green beans. I really want some bell peppers. I will probably forego carrots, lettuce, and corn. But this is just me musing as I write this piece. Come next week, who knows? Maybe some onions and a turnip or two, or, better yet, jalapenos, my favorite! Too, I wonder if I should bring in some sandy soil and grow a patch of peanuts. Or better yet, sunflowers! They get pretty tall. I wonder if they would get even taller in a keyhole garden?"

Growing that first keyhole garden was a hugely rewarding experience. I live in rural Texas which tends to make it easier to have one, I guess. But what about people in cities who are space deprived for a regular garden? Could they manage a keyhole garden? And what about people who are perhaps older and don't want to bend over so much (like I was getting to be, according to certain family members). They might like to have one.

I knew that I certainly wanted

another keyhole garden, but kept hitting a roadblock when it came to building one because of the dreaded task of dealing with rocks and cinder blocks again. I had used all the materials and spare parts that I had collected over the years and would have to obtain new ones, plus the time and physical labors spent building my first garden prompted me to keep putting it off.

I posed the question to my younger brother who, like me, enjoys inventing things. He was interested in the concept based on the tremendous success of my rock and cinder block garden, so we tried to come up with ideas on how to build keyhole garden containers that are quick and easy to install without too much labor. They would have to be durable, as well, and not cost too much for the parts.

It took us several weeks of trying this and trying that before we finally arrived at a prototype. It required very precise measurements on its stable of parts and our creating some innovative jigs in order for us to produce all the parts into the same approximate dimensions each time. The fudge-factor for the parts was very small.

That spring, we decided to build three or four new keyhole gardens based on these designs and place them near the original rock and cinder block garden for testing. We wanted to determine how long it takes to build one, what materials to use, and how they stand up over time. We also had some friends and relatives interested in the concept so we built some keyhole gardens for them, to add to our experimentation realm.

After about four years of advancing through the experimental stages, making changes here and there, and realizing that the durability horizon had been conquered, we began marketing keyhole garden kits under the name of keyholefarm.com, mainly in answer to so many people wanting us to build one for them. Keyhole gardens were becoming more popular among gardeners. After our website went up, we began shipping them throughout the United States.

The beauty of it all is that keyhole gardens allow people to have their own miniature farm, one that produces well and offers many positive attributes.

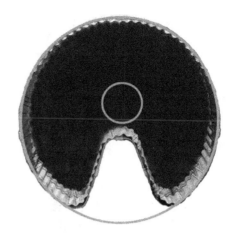

CHAPTER TWO
What Is A
Keyhole Garden?

A keyhole garden is circular in design, approximately six feet in diameter with a raised bed. From the circular perimeter, a wedge is made, similar to a piece of pie. A circular wire basket is placed at the tip of the wedge in the center of the garden, making it resemble an old-timey keyhole when viewed from above, looking down at it, thus the name.

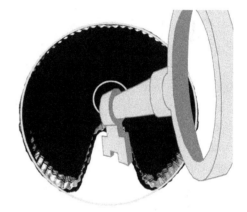

When filling the main raised-bed garden portion with content, I generally layer with wetted-down cardboard and other paper products, leaves, cut grass, small tree branches, compost, and other ingredients, mixing a little "green" material with quite a bit of "brown" material.

Then I usually put about a foot depth of topsoil as the top layer, water it in, let the level sink a little as some of the ingredients settle, then add more topsoil. The topsoil is angled down slightly from the taller interior basket

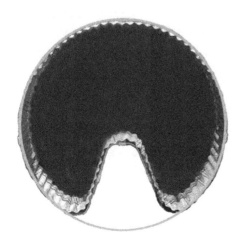

toward the outside of the garden.

The 12-inch diameter internal basket is used to "feed" the garden, via water and certain left-over foodstuffs, like banana peels, veggie cuttings, and coffee grounds. This basket is placed in the center of the garden and is a little higher than the main garden. Inside, the basket extends down to the ground. The idea is to provide moisture and minerals in this manner to embrace recycling through circulation, or leaching nutrients into the soil, that these nutrients drift toward the outer edges of the circular container.

With my gardens, I generally try to group crops, thinking ahead to allow greatest sun exposure as they grow, trying to avoid, for instance, huge squash leaves from overshadowing the spinach next to it. Most of my plantings are done by poking holes in the dirt about three inches apart and then going back and placing the seeds in those holes before covering them up and smoothing out the surface.

You can expect an "overflow" reaction as some plants grow over the sides and deposit their fruits on the ground. This has been my experience

with watermelons, pumpkins, various types of cucumbers, certain melons, cantaloupes, and several varieties of tomatoes, to name a few. Sometimes these crops grow inside the container, sometimes outside. I try to train the vines to meet my preferences for a particular crop.

Because I plant the seeds so close together, it is often quite an adventure to find the resultant crops when they are ready to pick, for the garden is thick with them. Here in Central Texas, I usually do a second round mid-summer by planting cowpeas and okra which tolerate hot weather better. It is amazing to watch these plants produce and reproduce many times during the hot months.

That's the general overview. Now let me backtrack slightly and provide a few of the details.

First, ingredients going into the main area of the keyhole garden are considered either brown or green.

Here is a list of a few common items that fall into those categories:

BROWNS *Carbon*

3-4 times as much as green:

Cardboard.

◆ Newspaper, phone books, junk mail.

Dry, yellow, or brown leaves and brown grass.

Dead, woody stalks or plants.

Sawdust, dryer lint.

Straw, wood ash from fireplaces (not a lot).

100% cotton, wool or silk.

GREENS *nitrogen*

Just need a little:

Kitchen scraps from veggies, melon rinds, eggshells, and fruit.

Coffee grinds and tea bags.

Freshly cut green leaves and grass clippings.

Manure

Coffee grinds with natural filters (coffee shops).

Fresh manure (barnyard kind)– avoid pet clinics.

I try to use a lot of wetted-down cardboard, mainly on the bottom. In my gardens the amount has varied depending upon how much cardboard I can collect. Cardboard is high in carbon, which plants crave, so use a lot of it. Newspapers, magazines, junk mail, telephone books, and catalogues fall into that same category. It decomposes fairly quickly and helps

attract good "bugs" to the garden, which assists in aeration and the conversion of paper into soil. I usually leave the strapping paper on boxes, mainly because it saves a lot of time and bugs tend to eat these strips, as well.

Wetting down the paper products helps provide a tighter seal and compresses the space they consume, making the fit into the main garden more compact.

The internal basket sits vertically at the tip of the wedge where access to it is maximized within the cut-out wedge area. Usually next to this basket I vertically place things like cardboard, paper products, and leaves, which minimizes dirt and other content from falling into the chicken-wire basket while filling the area next to it in the main garden.

Although it is far from being a hard-and-fast rule, the layers of Keyhole Farm gardens generally consist of cardboard/paper products on the bottom, followed by a layer of brown leaves, on top of which are placed sticks and twigs, old wood, and grass clippings mixed with some green material, followed by another layer of brown leaves perhaps mixed with some compost or manure, followed by another thin layer of greens, and then on the top more brown leaves.

I push down the top layer of brown leaves firmly and add more to the top if needed, then proceed to dump in topsoil, usually mixed with compost. The topsoil mashes down the top layer of leaves and falls into the nooks and crannies below. I put downward pressure on the topsoil as it is added and eventually form the top of the garden so that it slopes downward from the internal basket toward the edges. In most cases, I then thoroughly water it down and leave it overnight to settle, then go back the next day and add more topsoil, redesign the top, and plant the seeds. Sometimes on the final top layer I mix in some potting soil.

There are probably a thousand ways to configure the garden, perhaps many better than my method, but, so far, this has worked well at Keyhole Farm.

CHAPTER THREE
Setting Up Your Keyhole

One thing to consider when setting up your keyhole garden, i.e. the container, is to place it on level ground. Sometimes this means adjustments to the earth underneath, especially if it is to sit on a slope. Quite often, this can be accomplished by digging slightly into the earth on one side.

With the rock type of garden and depending upon the materials, it might just mean building up a side higher than the opposite side. On the other hand, with our keyhole garden kits it means adjusting the earth since the panels are all the same approximate height. Our kits consist of a metal frame, and then panels are attached to it extending beyond the frame's top and bottom. I usually establish level by constructing the frame first and wheeling it outside to the site and digging around it. It is a little easier to see where to dig utilizing the hollow metal frame as a guide. Then I place a long board across the top, put a level on the board, and pinpoint fairly level status, after which the frame is taken back inside and the panels are installed. The completed unit is then wheeled back outside and put into place on the altered ground.

When placing the keyhole garden on the ground, several additional matters might be considered. For instance, which way do you want it to face for optimum access to the keyhole's wedge for recycling? Where will it have best access to the sun, if that is preferred? Is access for those in wheelchairs provided with a workable pathway? And how will water be provided to the structure?

If more than one keyhole is being

installed, another question is what distance to place them apart from each other. Do you want space enough to get a lawnmower between them? Will enough space be provided for possible overflow of crops such as watermelons and pumpkins?

It can be helpful to determine answers to these questions when considering the general layout. Some of it is a guess, based upon crop choices; however, a few of these decisions are more rigid, depending upon the preference of the gardener.

KEYHOLE FARM GARDEN KITS ON EXHIBIT IN PARIS, FRANCE

There are some distinct advantages and disadvantages when it comes to choosing which type of keyhole garden container to utilize, the rock or the kit type. Rock gardens have a more rustic,

perhaps natural look to them, which can be very appealing. They are difficult to move once in place, which can be a positive or a negative aspect depending upon the situation.

Keyhole garden kits have a more modern look and come in different colors. In 2014, the French government purchased five kits from Keyhole Farm to be put on display during European heritage days in Paris. After the multi-day event, the gardens were to be relocated to the ministry of education for children to learn gardening. At the event, however, bamboo skirts were placed around the gardens because it was said they looked too industrial for a "heritage days" type of presentation.

There are a few distinct advantages of the kits:

(1) They are easy to put together, which can usually be accomplished in about an hour and a half.

(2) They are easy to disassemble and move to another location.

(3) When working in the garden, it is easier to get closer to the crops – you

do not have that extra eight inches of rock to reach over.

(4) They are lightweight and easily moved about prior to filling.

(5) For those with disabilities, the kits are very near ADA compliant in relationship to the 24-inch reach from outside the garden.

As this text is being written, Keyhole Farm produces two sizes of keyhole garden kits, the regular size which is six feet in diameter and a smaller mini-kitchen garden that is approximately 42 inches in diameter without a wedge.

The smaller version allows for the 24-inch reach all around it, whereas the regular sized garden comes to within about two inches next to the back of the internal basket of allowing the 24-inch reach, otherwise the rest of the garden is in ADA compliance.

With about an eight-inch stone border around rock gardens, the ADA compliance ability is greatly reduced.

The kit version is also accommodating for school-age children to participate in gardening as it is more amenable to their reach capacities.

gardens is planted with seeds, while the other five percent consists of transplants, mainly tomatoes.

CHAPTER FOUR
Organize Your Plants

Deciding what to plant is a daunting task, while at the same time an enjoyable one. At Keyhole Farm, I always select some tried and true crops that I enjoy to eat, but also extend the choices to include some exotics just to see how they do. Most seed companies provide information about when to plant them, how long it takes to make a crop, and details about how to care for them. Some need a lot of sun, some do not. The amount of water for a particular variety also often comes into play.

I usually try to vary the crops in a given garden, perhaps planting beans and corn together, in their own separate rows, one after the other, mainly because corn uses a lot of nitrogen and beans tend to put it back into the soil – balance.

About 95 percent of the space in my

On average, about five different types of crops are planted in a single garden, although this does vary depending on numerous factors, such as which seeds I have on hand and which crops I want to group together.

As a rule of thumb, I normally space the seeds about three inches apart. However, I do give transplants a little more space, and I take into consideration predicted leafing of some crops so that a different plant next to it is not totally covered with shade.

The ideal keyhole garden is lush with very little unused surface space.

In my keyhole gardens, I usually plant a few mammoth sunflower seeds near the internal basket in the middle. They can grow to nearly 20 feet tall. Their big leaves provide some intermittent shade to the plants below on blistering hot days. Too, they are magnificent to look at, their big yellow heads (which consist of seeds) attract

the all-important bees to the garden like a bright signal high in the air. Plus birds are attracted to eat the seeds.

Birds are a menace to pesky grasshoppers; plus the mockingbirds, doves, sparrows, and cardinals tend to focus on the sunflower seeds high above and largely leave undisturbed the tomato plants far below. At least, that's been my experience thus-far.

Of interest, during my second year of keyhole gardening after I had just finished planting my first garden from a kit, I had ventured to plant a pumpkin patch into the ground a distance from the keyholes. I mounded the dirt and inserted pumpkin and watermelon seeds in an area where an underground spring tended to keep the soil moist. It consisted of four long rows.

After the task had been done and I was journeying back to the house, I noticed on the return trip that there was a pumpkin seed remaining in the fold of a pocket in one of the packets. Rather than return to the patch, I simply stuck that seed into the new keyhole garden and covered it up, not really expecting much of it.

Soon, the seed erupted into a plant and as it grew in its early stages it was way ahead of the pumpkin seeds in the patch. Growth could be witnessed each day, with the leaves getting bigger and bigger. In comparison, the pumpkin patch plants looked quite wimpy. I asked Dr. Tolman who happened by one day how she would explain the differences in growth. She asked if the pumpkin seeds in the patch were planted in mounds, to which the answer was yes. She then explained that the entire keyhole garden represented the mound for that lone seed, with lots of elbow room for its root system, plus it was being fed each day as the nutrients and moisture in the internal basket leached their way through the soil, an example of the perfect system.

That one seed quickly overtook a large area of the lawn and produced some giant pumpkins. It was impressive!

I have planted numerous tomatoes, all sizes and many varieties, most of which have produced beyond what I had expected of them. Sometimes the vines work their way across the top of the keyhole garden, meandering their way among other plants. Often, they spill over the edge of the garden and produce huge crops of tomatoes on the side. And, at times, I install wire frames around the tomato plants and train them to grow tall and pretty much within this wire abode on top of the garden bed.

In 2015, the tomato crop was extremely good. Tomatoes of all sizes were planted in the various keyhole gardens in the early spring and produced crops until mid-summer when the 105-degree temperatures apparently stressed them too much.

Their production slowed considerably and most of the plants were pulled up to make way for other crops. I kept one of the plants that produced small, one-inch diameter tomatoes in one of my mini-gardens just to see what would happen. A few

of the branches had apparently died, having turned brown and fairly crisp. But by October, after the weather had cooled some, new green branches erupted from the dead branches and new growth had developed in the root branches. The count of new tomatoes was 88 by the end of the month, all from that one plant that normally I would have pulled up weeks before.

Among the list of successful crops that have been raised in my keyhole gardens in Central Texas are varieties of black-eyed peas (cowpeas), green beans, lettuces, squash, spinach, zucchini, cauliflower, carrots, corn, popcorn, cucumbers, cantaloupe, watermelons, pumpkins, spring wheat, bell peppers, jalapeno peppers, fava beans, English peas, early peas, banana melons, okra, asparagus, herbs, Swiss chard, sunflowers, garlic, serpent melons, tomatoes, onions, and many more.

with eyes. I waited until the upper part of the plants had died before digging them up to assure a large size. It was a great harvest.

I recently had a superb crop of potatoes, having planted about half of a keyhole garden with potato wedges

since they fare nicely in extremely hot weather and produce tremendously.

The okra plants grow very tall and produce fruit on their way up. They have to be picked almost daily because the pods grow so fast. When the pods are out of reach, it is simply a matter of bending the stalk down, cutting off the pod, and then letting the stalk spring back into place. The spring-back is probably beneficial since it vibrates the plant to promote its juices flowing and is akin to "spanking" tomato plants, rapping them gently with a rolled-up newspaper to provide a low-key, gentle vibration designed to promote growth, which I believe actually happens based on my experiences.

Part of the quest is to plant crops when they will produce best. In late May or early June I usually plant an abundance of black-eyed peas and okra

garden since time spent doing this task was an issue.

CHAPTER FIVE
Examples In Watering

One of the purposes of keyhole gardening is to use as little water as possible, which involves training the plants to thrive and survive as much as possible on moisture provided by the internal basket. One goal is to have the roots of the plants lean toward the basket and seek depth, which is part of the reason why the upper layer of the soil is sloped upward toward the basket, the planting of seeds at a slight angle.

However, inevitably some external water will be needed at times. With my first keyhole garden, the rock and cinder block variety, I watered using a water hose with a sprinkler head on it, as needed, depending upon how the plants looked. During the hotter weather, watering occurred about 15 minutes a day when it did not rain.

When I began adding gardens, I installed a watering system for each

My first sprinkler systems consisted of a half-inch PVC pipe extending up the internal basket with a sprinkler head that could be adjusted to pretty much just water the garden, as needed.

When more gardens were added, I began experimenting with quarter-inch macro-tubing with smaller sprinkler heads and later, through experimentation, developed an

underground watering system. The idea was that the sprinkler system could be used early-on while I was trying to germinate seeds and promote initial growth of the plants, and later the underground system could be used to draw the roots deeper and perhaps alleviate attacks by snails who are attracted to the remnants of exposed water.

With macro-tubing and small heads, the amount of water expended is minimal. I rigged the system to a timer that would automatically produce watering at night when the wind is less, therefore vastly reducing water loss due to evaporation.

One technique I utilized with the macro-tubing sprinkler system was to place the small heads around the upper rim of the internal basket, which used less quarter-inch tubing and shot water toward the exterior. At first, when there are no crops, the entire garden gets watered on top to help germinate the seeds. Then, as plants grow, their leaves block the water flow and most of the water stays near the basket, promoting roots to lean in that direction.

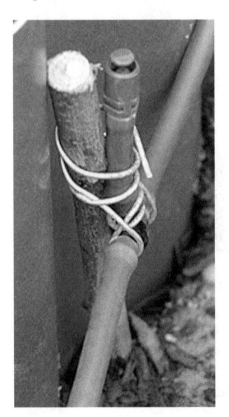

Although it is not helpful in training plants to not crave water when there is very heavy, continuously flooding rainfall, keyhole gardens tend to fare well when this occurs. I have talked to ground gardeners who quite often have to start all over when floods destroy the plants. With the raised bed keyhole gardens that drain fairly well, this has not been a problem.

CHAPTER SIX
Experiment With
Seed Germination

It never fails. Just after the holidays and in early January my spirits enliven with the desire to get a head start on spring planting. This means attempting to germinate seeds and start their growth indoors in anticipation of the last frost date. I collect seeds and can't wait to plant some of them in advance of spring.

For several years, the germination process I utilized was to fold a paper towel in half and then place seeds on half of the folded-over portion. Then I would fold the empty half over the part with seeds, water it down, carefully slide the dampened towel into a plastic bag, squeeze the air out, seal it, and then hang it in front of a window or in a warm place. Eventually, some seeds would germinate, but it often took days, even weeks, for this to happen.

In 2015, I was gifted a Christmas present -- a soda machine that contained a carbonated water attachment to perhaps save me a little money on soft drinks. Knowing that plants crave carbon, I had a bright idea -- I used carbonated water on the paper towels instead of tap water. Most of the seeds germinated within a 24-hour to 36-hour time period. In researching the results, I learned that the use of carbonated water can often produce bigger plants with quicker growth. Therefore, at times, I began using a sprinkler can to water plants in the gardens with carbonated water.

I utilized my newfound quick germination process with carbonated water to provide seeds now ready to be planted in the garden bed. I surrounded the seeds in the bed with a small amount of sand. They produced wonderfully. I had a good crop of black-eyes by the date that I would normally first plant the seeds. They grew faster than usual and produced some great crops.

As an added experiment, I had in previous years attempted to plant black-eyed peas in the early spring only to have the seeds rot prior to germination. They apparently required warmer weather for the germination to begin, which was not happening in early spring. In hotter weather they do splendidly.

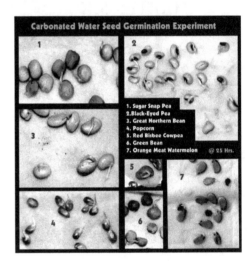

Carbonated Water Seed Germination Experiment

1. Sugar Snap Pea
2. Black-Eyed Pea
3. Great Northern Bean
4. Popcorn
5. Red Bisbee Cowpea
6. Green Bean
7. Orange Meat Watermelon   @ 25 Hrs.

The other seeds that were germinated utilizing the same carbonated water method also sprang up quicker and stronger. These included sugar snap peas, Great Northern beans, popcorn (out of a bag), the Red Brisbee cowpea, green beans (including pintos), and yellow meat watermelon seeds.

CHAPTER SEVEN
The Birds and the Bees

Bees are my friends, a necessary ingredient in keyhole gardening. It is reassuring when journeying through the mass of keyholes in the early morning hours to see that bees are busy pollinating the blooms of the plants.

To encourage bee participation and selection of my gardens as new stomping grounds, I usually plant a few flowers, like morning glories, as an added way to attract them. Since my debut into keyhole gardening, I am yet to be stung by a bee. They tend to focus on their business and I on mine,

sort of a co-existence.

Here in Central Texas the bees usually conduct their business in the morning hours, and as the day heats up, it's time for the yellow jackets and red wasps to do theirs.

Throughout the day, especially in the late spring and summer after they hatch out, beautiful butterflies roam about playing tag with their brothers and sisters and landing on the leaves of the plants.

I also try to attract birds, partially because the location of Keyhole Farm is in a residential area that does not allow chickens. Birds can assist in alleviating grasshoppers that tend to come in waves that last a few days, rather sporadically, sometimes not at all. This is one reason I plant mammoth sunflowers, a favorite perch and meal for the winged creatures. They fill up on sunflower seeds and tend to leave my tomatoes alone.

I have noticed that bees seem to like dry weather. During times when we have had days of continuous rain their numbers are noticeably down.

It is amazing to spend time in the garden area watching the insect world unfold, learning their traits, and enjoying the beauty of their excursions. They very much operate in their own little universe, one that is regularly ignored by the human population, but

an amazing, mesmerizing one to experience.

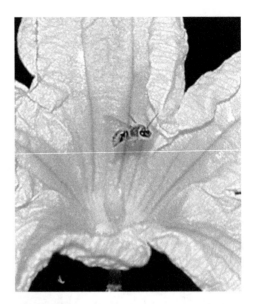

CHAPTER EIGHT
Predator Control

Having a keyhole garden is akin to developing a beautiful and sustaining vegetable smorgasbord, with homegrown crops that are delicious to eat and, perhaps beyond that, safe.

Most of Keyhole Farm's crops are of an heirloom variety, the seeds handed down generation to generation, tried, proven, and true to produce crops of maximum nutrition. Part of this tremendous gain in nutrition comes from harvesting the crops at their peak, when they have spent additional time gaining nutritious values from the soil, exceeding crops that are purchased at grocery stores, since the latter are often picked early to assure longer shelf life. Stores pretty much have to do this for their produce sections to survive, so it is not necessarily a bad thing. Unfortunately, their veggies are often bland tasting, and you never know for sure where they came from, what was used on them (i.e. toxic chemicals), and the point on the timeline that gains in nutritional value was cut off when they were removed from the soil.

The value-based smorgasbord in the keyhole is very attractive to humans; however, the keyhole salad dish is also attractive to other mammals, predators which can't resist such an oasis of wonderful food. The list of potential predators is quite long and each will likely require its own method of alleviation. Here are some examples of predators that Keyhole Farm has dealt with over the years and methods utilized that could perhaps be mirrored for reducing visits from similar types of predators.

The first one I encountered was not a giraffe, bear, or lion, but a mere kitty cat that chose one of my keyholes in which to lounge during the day. The cat had its own spot where vines and leaves would get mashed down during the cat's nap, where he would spend most of the day sleeping on top of them. The remedy was to place upright a few sticks in the soil in that area. The cat went away.

A few years ago I had some magnificent yellow-meat watermelon vines that had grown over the side of one of my keyhole garden onto the ground. A variety of sizes of watermelons were growing, two of which were very large, three were mid-sized, and about five that were small, about fist-sized. I noticed one morning that the smaller ones had vanished. My thinking at first was that I had perhaps simply miscounted. The next morning I noticed some teeth marks in the rinds of two of the larger melons. One of the mid-sized melons was half-eaten with about half of the inner portion remaining. The watermelons were definitely under attack.

I shoved the half-eaten melon into a wire-construction live trap and covered the larger slightly damaged melons, for protection, with a wire lid made from some old fencing materials on hand. When I checked the trap the next day, nothing. On the second day, I had caught an opossum, about mid-sized and very cute. When I approached the trap, he was not very happy and moved about some, hissing a little. I stood over him and finally received his facial attention. I explained to him that although no signs had been posted saying "no opossums allowed," the garden was not intended for him to raid. I told him that I considered it a compliment that he would choose my garden over all the others, but that he would have to feed elsewhere. Then I opened the trap and let him go. He ran toward a bunch of trees in the distance and disappeared. I had hoped that his being caught and my lecture had provided enough discouragement for him not to return.

It didn't work. Two days later another raid. Another of the mid-sized watermelons was partially eaten.

I repeated the live trap procedure and the next morning there he was, the same opossum caught again. I relocated him out in the country a few miles away, with the landowners' permission.

The year after that incident another raid occurred. I had grown what I considered to be a prize pumpkin. It lay on the ground next to the keyhole from where its vines protruded. The pumpkin was huge, nearly perfect in shape, and had turned a bright orange, about a week away from picking. Two days later I made the rounds and came to the place the pumpkin was supposed to be. It was not there. The first thought was that someone had stolen it.

As I ambled around the garden I noticed that on the ground inside the wedge was where it lay, about a fourth of its top eaten away. The first thought was that the culprit must have been another 'possum, but I questioned how such a small critter could move that pumpkin that far. It was very heavy.

I again brought out the live trap, loaded it with a small sliver of the giant pumpkin as bait, and picked up the remainder of the pumpkin and set it inside the keyhole, about waist high, to get it out of reach of the predator that I expected would return.

When I checked the next day, the trap had not been sprung and the bait was still inside, but the remainder of the pumpkin itself that was placed inside the keyhole was missing. A search found it a distance from the garden under a pecan tree, just the bottom rind, shaped like a bowl, remaining. Too, I found that in one of my gardens about half the black-eyed peas had been chomped off, leaving behind five-inch-long, nearly bald stalks. That's when I noticed deer droppings nearby and realized that in another area of my property pears on the lower branches of the tree had also been robbed, with tell-tale deer droppings on the tree's perimeter, as well.

During those days, Central Texas had been experiencing a drought with brown grass covering the ground. The days had been very hot, registering over 100 degrees. My keyhole gardens were lush with a forest green tint, in stark contrast to the ocean of brittle grass upon which they floated. I had occasionally seen white-tail deer roaming at night on the edge of town, but as far as I knew, they had never ventured this deeply into a residential neighborhood, having to bypass several houses to arrive at my site.

Although this is subject to change, I had chosen to not fence off my gardens, to keep them open for easier public view and to better enable photography of them for my website. But the deer made us rethink that option.

As an interim measure I decided to scatter about half-a-dozen solar-powered lights on the edge of the garden region. I also pieced together "L"-shaped PVC with the long edge buried into the edge of some of my gardens onto which on the short end that stuck outside the garden I placed a short dangling string and tied it to a CD. As the wind blew at night the CD would flutter and reflect light from the solar lights, perhaps given deer pause to enter.

The third thing I did was to hammer into the ground some waist-high wooden stakes at the corners of the garden area and through eyelets screwed into the wood near the top string fishing line designed to outline the garden area. At the end of the fishing line was placed metal noise-makers (tin cans and junk pieces of conduit) that would be loud when pulled off an upside down five-gallon bucket onto which they were stacked, should something venture across the fishing line, come in contact with the line, and force the noisemakers off the bucket.

So far, this remedy has worked. Like a fisherman, I check my lines each morning. Occasionally they have been tripped, but not usually. The deer problem, at least at the time of this writing, has apparently been solved without having to build a fence or experiment with other means.

Other predators that have been problematic at times are of the insect variety. Most bugs that grow inside of keyhole gardens are beneficial, you could almost say necessary, for adequate aeration of the soil and the decomposition of the cardboard and other materials placed inside. However, there are exceptions.

Three that have caused us problems at times are snails, squash bugs, and fire ants.

My garden area is prone to having snails. When spring hits and they first appear, I try to gather them up wherever I find them and either crush them or place them in a container for disposal. Eventually, they are not as plentiful, which helps especially when new plantings are trying to come up. Once a plant is larger, with bigger leaves, snails can nibble holes in the leaves but do not usually destroy the plants if their presence is taken care of in short order. Snails can live for five years, so it is an ongoing process. They tend to come out more in wet weather or when sprinkler systems are running in the gardens. Sometimes I dust the base of the keyholes with food-grade diatomaceous earth (a powdery substance that is considered safe for humans to consume, but you don't want to breathe it in). It works like broken glass on snails and grasshoppers when they come in contact with it, ripping at their undersides. DE does not work well when it gets wet, so timing is important.

I usually plant squash (which includes zucchini, crook-neck, and pumpkins mainly) about three times a year, separately for the spring, summer, and fall gardens. In the summer and fall plantings, squash bugs are a minor problem, if at all, but in the spring they replicate fast and can destroy the plants

and crops in short order. My methods of control include spreading diatomaceous earth when possible, but usually just hand-picking them off the vines and crushing them.

Sometimes I take a portable shop-vac and suck them into it if they are plentiful.

I also inspect the underside of the big leaves to see if they have laid their eggs, which resemble small BBs neatly arranged in a compact configuration. I crush the BBs with my fingers to wipe out the up-and-coming new generation of these gray bugs.

Occasionally, a tribe of fire ants decides to inhabit a keyhole garden. Their entry is usually up the side, and their domicile is in that neighborhood.

Usually the dirt there is piled up and disturbed on top, so they are easy to spot.

What I do is to take a stick and poke it in the ant-laden area and along the entryway up the side of the garden.

Then I heavily sprinkle diatomaceous earth into the holes and upon the surrounding area, plus along their entryway and on the ground just outside the keyhole.

Sometimes I stir the top area of inhabitation with the stick and put more DE on top.

Usually in a couple of days they are gone, and I have not used hazardous chemicals to take care of the matter.

I always try to use natural remedies in my gardens.

stays with them always, as does the know-how of sustaining nature and themselves.

CHAPTER NINE
Education and Adventure

In the old days children helped on the family farm. They learned about crops and helped in the gardens and in the fields. As time passed, this occurred at a lesser degree, to the point that now youngsters seldom go near a farm and they know next to nothing about plants, especially how to raise them. Many do not experience the feeling of success that comes with planting seeds and seeing the results as plants grow. They spend their spare time playing with cell phones and other electronic devices.

Keyhole gardening offers an opportunity for youths to experience a whole new universe with a mini-farm in their own backyard and can provide a background of learning that extends itself to the survival element, caring for the earth, and learning about fruits, vegetables, and the soil. The extra knowledge of cooperating with nature

Several school districts, mainly in southern states, have taken up this challenge by setting up keyhole gardens at their schools for experimentation and educational purposes. The first school to order keyhole garden kits from Keyhole Farm installed six of them, to include geography, science, mathematics, and economics as they pertain to agriculture in the keyhole curriculum.

Youngsters have visited the Keyhole Farm experiment station to help with planting and to learn about how the perfect system actually works.

For instance, some Girl Scouts

participated in spring planting as part of their Feed The World project.

At first, they were somewhat timid, but before the end of the day they were confidently digging in the dirt, playing with insects, and offering suggestions as to what to plant where like old farmers. They thoroughly enjoyed the visit and were excited when about a week later they returned. They would point at a sprouting plant and say, "I planted that one, and that one, and that one...."

One of Keyhole Farm's customers set up her garden in the early spring and grew several crops, mainly onions, herbs, and beans. Later in the year toward the end of fall, she prepared Halloween pumpkins for her daughters to be carved utilizing the traditional method and dumped the guts and seeds that had been scraped out of the middle of the pumpkins into the internal basket of her keyhole garden for recycling. The next spring she noticed a strange plant coming out of the area next to the basket, thinking it was perhaps squash, which she had not planted.

Eventually, the mystery was solved as pumpkins started growing and overflowing over the edges of the garden container into the backyard in all directions. The large, beautiful pumpkins totaled 18 in number from the one seed that had made its way into the soil. Her three daughters were thrilled when looking out at the massive garden and enjoyed bragging about their unique "pumpkin patch" to their friends. They learned some things about gardening in the process, another education example.

Whenever a new product is introduced at Keyhole Farm, such as the recent Mini-Keyhole Kitchen Garden, instruction sheets must be written.

I always wonder if these instructions are complete enough, or if explanations need to be revised. One thing we try to do to ascertain the efficiency and completeness of the instruction sheets is to persuade someone from an objective point of view to try them out and tell us if an element is not clear enough.

In the case of the mini-garden kit, I asked my granddaughter, at the time a sophomore in high school who had minimal experience with tools and this type of construction, to put a kit together based on the newly drafted instructions.

She agreed to do it. After being coached on how to use a power drill she took the printed instruction sheets

and began, all on her own.

This involved putting together the frame, screwing the tees attached to the tee posts to the curved pieces and then proceeding to install panels onto the frame. Afterward, she constructed the wire internal basket.

In all, it took her about an hour-and-a-half to complete the project, of which she got a rush admiring her finished product. She did note a couple of revisions that she thought would improve the instruction sheets, which we made.

Interestingly, during the next two years of high school she undertook some fairly elaborate and complicated class projects involving the use of tools. She drew up the plans, knowing they could be built, partially because she knew she had the ability to do so.

At one time I was involved in drilling water wells with my father and grandfather. We also cleaned out wells, did some plumbing, and erected windmills.

We used a cable-tool rig called a Fort Worth Spudder to do the drilling, which could take days of punching a straight hole in the earth. A lot of sweat and manual labor was utilized, but eventually there was a giant rush when we hit water and turned on the faucets. Just seeing the plentiful clean water filling the buckets provided a tremendous feeling of accomplishment.

As part of the process I learned a lot about hydraulics, which in later life was invaluable to me in becoming a state-licensed irrigator.

The point is that sometimes what you learn at an earlier age will impact your future.

This is yet another educational example of what keyhole gardening and all the elements that go into it can provide.

What students learn today can be built upon.

They might recognize innovations never before considered.

By having an understanding and background in gardening, their ability to create is vastly enhanced.

To me, teaching students to be creative in a positive manner is to be applauded.

"Keyhole gardens are a unique way to raise crops in that they conserve water, minimize backbreaking work, and provide little or no weeding.

"Most keyholes utilize rocks or cinder blocks and take hours to construct. Our models are semi-portable, fairly easy to disassemble and move. They weigh about 46 pounds.

"With the thin side panels, gardeners can get closer to the crops in these raised beds, making them easier for the handicapped to enjoy.

"It takes my staff about an hour to an hour-and-a-half to put these kits together, although this is subject to the skills of the person doing it.

"Keyhole Farm gardens are durable, with a six-year track record (as of 2014) and likely much longer.

"Tools needed are a power screwdriver or drill and a rubber mallet or something similar. Other  things useful, but optional, are a level, work gloves, and shears or scissors.

CHAPTER TEN
Answers To FAQs

This last chapter of the book is dedicated to a description of Keyhole Farm, LLC garden kits, including answers to some FAQs (frequently asked questions).

The 2015 Keyhole Farm brochure answers many of them:

"Our gardens consist of a metal frame made of galvanized metal tubing, specifically bent into three different configurations that provide an upper and lower rail separated by vertical posts. They are connected with especially designed PVC tees that are firmed up with screws.

"Construction can be done indoors, then rolled or carefully carried to the garden location. Nylon ties are included for use in installing panels. When completed, the frame measures approximately six feet in diameter with a wedge indented inward. Height is approx. 28.5 inches when panels are added.

"The sides consist of 12 panels (regular keyhole garden kit). These are made of ridged polycarbonate that measure in height 28.5 inches (approx.).

"Holes in the siding are pre-drilled for use in attaching nylon ties to the metal frame or to adjoin siding panels.

"The panels slightly overlap as they are assembled, with the ridges running vertically. Panel colors come in castle gray, red brick, and forest green.

"Inside the keyhole garden sits a vertical one-foot wide (approx.) wire mesh cage (about eight inches in diameter with the mini-garden). This cage extends several inches above the height of the garden. It is used to feed the garden with table scraps, for instance.

"The internal basket is important because it provides natural nutrients for the crops, along with added moisture as its contents decompose and are circulated throughout the garden.

"Keyhole Farm recently introduced its Mini-Keyhole Kitchen Garden. It is a scaled-down version of the regular keyhole, about half the size in content, with no wedge. Several people had inquired about a smaller garden due to space considerations, plus this is a garden that easily meets ADA standards for the handicapped in wheelchairs.

"According to our measurements, it takes about 1.8 yards of fill (which includes soil and other materials) to accommodate a regular keyhole garden, whereby the mini-garden takes about .81 yards. The mini-garden consists of six panels, 10 curved pieces of galvanized metal tubing for the frame, and five vertical posts with tees pre-attached. Screws, ties, and parts for the internal basket are included."

Answers to other frequently asked questions include these:

1. Detailed construction instructions are included with the kit.
2. The main reason for the internal basket is to put food scraps (like banana and orange peels, rinds, shelled greens, tea bags, coffee grounds, and other "green" materials) inside for leaching throughout the soil. It is important to keep this basket fairly full to obtain maximum benefit.

3. The gardens hold up well in both winter and summer. The manufacturers of the polycarbonate side panels have declared that they are safe.

4. Do you have local distribution centers in other states? The answer is "not many." My kits are sold online slightly above wholesale in order to keep the cost to customers way down. To add up to 50 percent in the cost for retail outlets is yet to happen.

5. Where are the kits made? They are manufactured in Central Texas. Keyhole Farm is a very small business that hand-tools each kit, conducts triple inspections, and ships mainly via United Parcel Service. Local pick-up of orders at our plant to save in shipping costs does occur, but because the company does not have regular retail business hours, an estimated time of arrival to pick up an order is requested. We also conduct tours of the experiment station.

6. Do you ship outside the United States? Answer: yes, we can; however, shipping costs can run more than the product itself, depending upon which country.

7. Will you conduct a keyhole gardening program for my garden club? The answer: We try to, if it will fit into our production schedule and your schedule of meetings.

8. Will a kit fit into my car? The answer: Probably. As of this writing, the boxes measure 30"x30"x7".

9. How long does it take to ship? The answer: as of this writing, kits usually ship within two days. Arrival time normally depends upon distance from our plant.

Keyhole gardeners should check with local, area, or state agricultural agencies for tips on what to plant and when, since seasons and adaptable plants vary somewhat by zones. Several magazines, such as *Texas Gardener* here in the Lone Star State, offer the same information, along with feature articles about gardening techniques and success stories. Other references are located on the keyholefarm.com website, including recommended books, DVDs, and online videos. The website also provides regular updates of what is happening at the experiment station, archived blogs, plus hundreds of photos.

The website offers the capability of ordering kits, including the regular size, mini-kitchen size, or simply the galvanized frame if customers want to add a different type of siding.

In summary, keyhole gardens are

unique. They represent a near-perfect system, with natural nutrients feeding the soil and ultimately the plants and crops from an internal basket. Gardeners have considerable control of the soil, partially because it is segregated from the ground. By planting a variety of crops, balance in the soil can be perfected resulting in very high-grade harvests.

Weeding is minimal, if at all; water is conserved due to just the garden being watered; much of the backbreaking work associated with traditional ground gardening is eliminated; and crops can be planted in a more compact manner, closer together than in a traditional garden.

Keyhole gardeners also have the advantage of harvesting crops at their peak. Soil that is aerated by small natural microorganisms, bugs, and worms provides growth elements and nourishment of the plants. These attributes are increased exponentially each day a plant remains in touch with the soil up until that peak moment. Therefore, harvests conducted at their peak result in much tastier and more nourishing crops.

As consumers, keyhole gardeners have nearly total control of the vegetables they feed to their families, which, in an era when GMOs have invaded many marketplaces and restaurants, can make a huge positive influence on diet and health.

Teaching youngsters how to grow

their own crops is important, as it provides not only a challenge but also confidence in how Mother Nature operates.

Keyhole gardeners begin with barren soil, but very quickly advance to plumes of green and soon to lush, miniature jungles loaded with healthy food that gives and keeps on giving.

There is something magic about raising some of your own crops, turning your hands into plowshares and learning about a key element of survival. Now, with keyholes, you can turn a corner of your own backyard into a showcase that has its roots deeply buried in something you created and nurtured.

ABOUT THE AUTHOR

W. Leon Smith has had a varied career, as a newspaper publisher, investigator, author, landscaper, water well driller, state-licensed irrigator, a multi-term mayor, and much more. One of his passions is keyhole gardening and producing kits so that others can experience the satisfaction of raising some of their own crops.

The intention of this book is to provide a general overview of the keyhole gardening concept, including various details that pertain to the adventures and challenges associated with keyholes that he has experienced after several years of participating in this endeavor.

He has been published in newspapers and magazines worldwide, including appearances in the *British Journalism Review* and in the documentary film, *Crawford, Texas*. He was featured in *The New York Times* and in *Vanity Fair*, to name only a few.

The author is currently working on several additional books and a 3D historical video. In print are these books:

The Switch Pitcher

What happens when a young baseball player, out of necessity, learns to pitch both right- and left-handed? This novelette explores his techniques and the challenges that erupt on and off the field when he becomes "ambi-disastrous" on the mound.

Although written with a younger readership in mind, baseball fans of all ages find *The Switch Pitcher* thrilling, as they do with the five bonus short stories.

Aldo Vidali, an 84-year-old collaborator of one of cinema's greatest directors: Federico Fellini, wrote a review of the first edition of *The Switch Pitcher*, and urged it be made into a motion picture. "Children, parents, and grandparents would flock to see such a movie," he said.

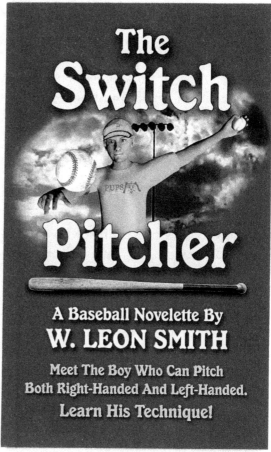

Among the bonus features is a short story about a sunflower living in a keyhole garden that literally "comes to life."

The second short story is a non-fiction account of an encounter with a UFO wherein the subject about thirty years later recounts details of the event while under hypnosis.

In the feature entitled ROD & REEL SNAPSHOTS, the author recounts unique fishing expeditions.

Another non-fiction entry is about growing up with a magical teddy bear named Fleddie Peddie.

The fifth short story, entitled PERIPHERAL ACCELERATON, is about an elderly man who is a perfectionist. He shares his extreme attention to detail with a friend, proving, for instance, the idea that it is extremely intelligent people who become carsick. He also recounts what it is truly like to be a time traveler.

This book is available at Amazon or by ordering at smithmediainc.com.

43

Epitaph

The Viet Nam war has just ended, but the military now wants to embark on its third quest to acquisition even more farm and ranch land for special maneuvers in this traditionally agricultural region of Central Texas. Acquisition could mean the destruction of small cities, cemeteries, and the lives of its inhabitants who have toiled and cared for the land for generations.

The landowners decide to form a coalition to fight the corporate/military land grab which they feel is unnecessary and they enlist the aid of a newcomer to their midst, a young black man who is trying to put into action Martin Luther King's "dream" in a region where the influence of the "Klan" still lingers. He wants to do his part to break the chains of a nation yet in turmoil.

The young man has started a weekly newspaper called *The Epitaph* in one of the small cities and finds himself embroiled in an emotional roller coaster after he befriends an elderly rancher whose life is etched into the homeland.

This epic novel is loosely based on actual events. Its setting begins at the turn of the 20th century with the rise of King Cotton and quickly evolves into modern times where issues of sovereignty of the land abound and questions about state-of-the-art weaponry in order to keep the military industrial complex profitable are explored.

Featuring adventure, romance, and intriguing characters, the tear-jerk ending lives up to the title.

This book is available at Amazon or by ordering at smithmediainc.com.

The Vigil – 26 Days In Crawford, Texas

In August of 2005, a grieving mother and her supporters laid siege to Crawford, Texas. Cindy Sheehan was determined to learn why her son had been killed in Iraq and wanted to ask the President himself, who refused to speak with her.

The result of the coverage of her vigil is a high-stakes, blow-by-blow account of the events that unfolded, including both sides of the controversy as provided by W. Leon Smith and his staff at *The Lone Star Iconoclast*.

Readers experience the volatile protests right along with the writers and participants: the heat, the fire ants, the gunplay, the celebrity appearances, and the intense rollercoaster.

Smith compiled the book after he was approached by peace officers who asked for use of some of the thousands of photographs taken by his staff to be used to train other officers on how to successfully keep an emotionally charged controversy such as this from getting out of hand. Their instructions would be used as a guide for peaceful protests, which this one evolved into. Smith decided to put into book form the events his newspaper covered, also as a type of schoolbook testimony for potential protestors

to read and learn from, a "this is how it's done" primer.

The Iconoclast had covered the event hour by hour and constantly posted the reports and interviews on its website, which at that time, was a new concept.

Later, Smith assisted in the translation of the book into Japanese.

The book was published by The Disinformation Company in New York, of which Smith has a number of copies. If anyone wants to obtain a copy, send an e-mail request to books@smithmediainc.com. They are also available at Amazon.

BONUS

Author's Note

The author of *Plant Your Garden In A Keyhole* has consented to have republished from his novelette, *The Switch Pitcher*, a keyhole garden short story. It is entitled "The Triffidzoid." A triffidzoid in this story is a raised-bed keyhole garden. The "zoid" applies to the design of the garden container consisting of circles and triangles and the "triffid" refers to a plant that was the subject of a novel, *The Day of the Triffids*, published in 1951 by John Wyndham, and a British film based on the novel in 1962.

The author of this short story was a youngster when the 1962 sci-fi horror film starring Howard Keel came out. The youth decided to give the movie a try, loading up on popcorn and soda while settling in at the indoor Texan Theatre in Hamilton, Texas on a Saturday while his mother and younger sister journeyed to San Marcos to visit Aquarena Springs as a Girl Scout trip and his father was tied up as production superintendent at a printing plant that day.

While buying his theatre ticket he was presented with a small packet of "triffid" seeds as a promotion. He never planted them because if they really were triffid seeds, the triffids might come and get him. They looked like sunflower seeds.

The Triffidzoid

Okay. Let me begin. This is a fictional account of what really happened.

I had spent several hours playing with and tending the plants in my keyhole gardens at Keyhole Farm. Like most good farmers, I talk to the plants, telling them how good they are, admiring their beauty, and encouraging them to produce good crops. I try to pull the bad bugs off their leaves, such as snails, and let the plants watch as I toss these slugs onto a concrete sidewalk where often they go "splat."

A keyhole garden has a raised bed about waist high which eliminates much of the backbreaking work gardeners often deal with. Keyhole gardens are round, six feet in diameter, except for a wedge being cut out, at which point inside the garden is placed a tall internal one-foot diameter wire basket for recycling leftovers. It is similar to a cylinder. These help to feed the garden with water and nutrients. They are called keyholes because if you look at them from a bird's-eye view they resemble old-timey keyholes. Many consider these gardens as the perfect gardening system, and I agree.

Sunflowers grow well in my keyholes because they know I respect and like them. I do not call them weeds, as some gardenauts do. I consider them friends.

The other day, these mammoth sunflowers started blooming. Since yellow is my favorite color I couldn't help but look at them and smile. They are called sunflowers, I guess, because their heads resemble mini-suns.

Anyway, after a long day I retired to my recliner in front of the TV and decided to choose a movie to watch. I was still thinking of the sunflowers some, so I chose to watch a movie, *Day of the Triffids*, about a similar plant, creatures that (according to the movie poster) "...they grow...know...walk...talk...stalk...and KILL!" I couldn't decide whether to watch the older version starring Howard Keel or the one I had recorded several years later on PBS (Public Broadcasting System). The show was a British mini-series based on the John Wyndham book. So, naturally, I chose to watch them both.

It was getting late and toward the end of my second movie, the later British version, I dozed off, only to be awakened by a noise outside the room, possibly in the yard. It sounded like movement and a strange voice crying "ouch." I thought it was probably my imagination, but I deemed it might be a burglar or someone needing help so rather than keep thinking about it I grabbed my flashlight and went to investigate.

As I ruled out things in my pathway, I eventually journeyed outside to the Keyhole Farm experiment station. Everything seemed in order, until the beam from my flashlight passed over the top of Alicia, one of my 11 keyhole gardens, most having components of a zoid (circles and triangles) in their construction. The biggest giant sunflower plant, the one I had talked to a few hours earlier and told him that he was taller than the rest and was looking good, was missing.

I shined the light onto the turf area inside the raised bed where the sunflower's roots had been and found the dirt loose and spread about.

"Someone has stolen my sunflower plant," I thought.

It was very quiet outside, no breeze at all. As I swung around I heard something near a chain-link fence in the distance on the edge of my property, as though movement had occurred, so I ventured in that direction, hoping to perhaps alarm a stray cat. I took giant steps over the gourd and pumpkin vines that had spewed out of adjoining keyhole gardens and were trailing on the ground.

As I pointed the light beam toward the sound I noticed slight movement again. I raised the flashlight and on its ascent soon caught the miniature sun...the face of the big sunflower... staring at me as he leaned against the fence. I went closer.

"What are you doing over here?" I asked, not expecting an answer.

The sunflower moved a few of its branches, as if lifting both shoulders and releasing them, an "I don't know" or "Who? Me?" movement. Then the plant replied in a deep gravely whisper, "I guess I went for a walk."

"Plants don't talk," I said.

"Well, not in the daytime," said my friend," but sometimes we whisper among ourselves at night."

"So you walked over here?" I asked, disbelievingly, "with your roots as feet?"

"Usually we are content to stay put," the plant said. "I am so much taller than the other plants that I wanted to see my friends' faces. From up there I can only see the tops of their heads."

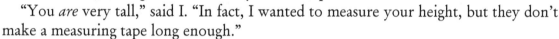

"You *are* very tall," said I. "In fact, I wanted to measure your height, but they don't make a measuring tape long enough."

"Let me make a suggestion," said the plant. "When we are very small, loosely tie a very long string around our necks and as we grow, the string will follow us up. Put distance markings on the string in advance, then simply read them off as we grow. Just be careful to not get the string tangled up with other plants."

"Hmm," I said. "I never thought of that."

"It will soon be difficult for me to walk," said the plant, "for my head is about to get heavy – lots of brains, you know – and the upper stalk will arch, making balance nearly impossible."

"That's probably just a few days away," I said.

"The arch is already starting," he replied.

"I just got through watching a movie, *Day of the Triffids*, about plants that cause 'spine chilling terror' according to promotional material. Do plants really stalk and kill?"

"Not sunflowers, although we do resemble Triffids somewhat. I say that, but the other day I did spit a sunflower seed at a squash bug and knocked him off a leaf. He was all right, though, just dazed a little."

I had another question. "Did I hear you yell 'ouch'?"

The sunflower smiled. "I nearly stumbled over the keyhole garden named 'Belle.' It's dark out and I forgot she was right there. I lost a lower branch and a leaf in the process. Didn't hurt too badly."

"Do you want me to help you get replanted in 'Alicia'? I asked.

"Actually," said the sunflower, "I prefer to do it myself. I jumped down out of the keyhole's raised bed earlier and think I can catapult myself back into it without doing a cartwheel. It's something I need to figure out in the event I decide to try to take a walk again. One thing, though. There are several sunflowers in 'Alicia' and not as many in the garden named 'Key-Rex.' Maybe I should relocate. It might make better use of the feeding that is done through the interior basket. 'Alicia' is pretty maxed out."

"It's okay with me," I said. "Just don't disturb the lower plants. That pumpkin takes up a lot of room and the zucchini is hogging the middle area. I'm not sure there's a slot big enough for you."

"I will look around and see," said the sunflower. Then the sunflower let out a huge yawn, which I took as a signal that he wanted to be alone.

"I'm going back inside," I said. "Take care of yourself."

The next thing I realized is that it was morning. I did my usual getting-up chores, knowing that I had several dreams the night before but couldn't remember any of them. I eventually ventured into the back yard. My big sunflower plant was missing. I couldn't believe it. Then I asked myself, "What's it doing over there?" It had been moved to the Key-Rex garden, if that was the same plant, which I felt sure it was.

To this day, I do not know how it got there.

This Planting Worksheet Might Be Helpful As You Decide What And Where To Plant In Your Keyhole Garden.

PLANTING WORKSHEET

INSTRUCTIONS:

On the numbered blanks below fill in the name of a crop. Then section off the circle at right and insert the number applicable to a crop in that area. Use a pencil in case you need to erase.

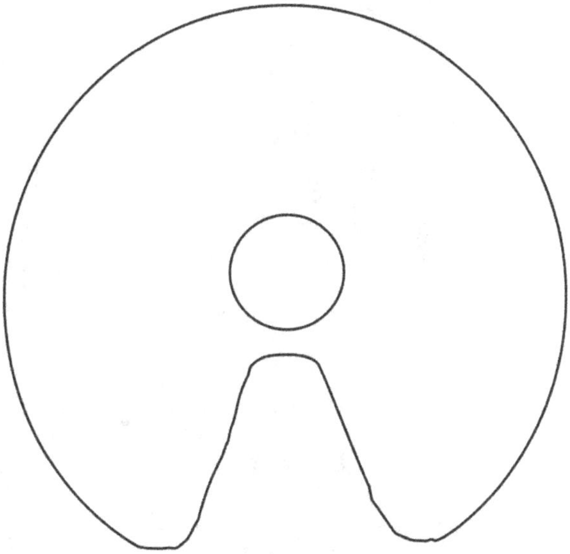

Crop		Planting Date
01.		
02.		
03.		
04.		
05.		
06.		
07.		
08.		
09.		
10.		
11.		
12.		

Keyhole Name or #:

Crop		Planting Date
13.		
14.		
15.		
16.		
17.		

Notes:

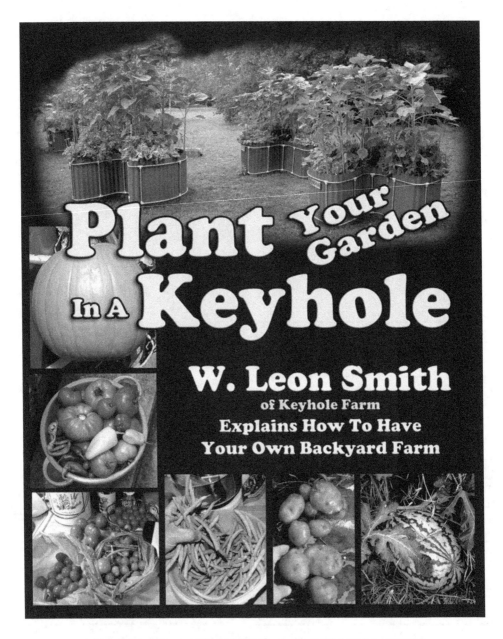

Plant Your Garden In A Keyhole

W. Leon Smith
of Keyhole Farm
Explains How To Have
Your Own Backyard Farm

TO ORDER A KEYHOLE GARDEN KIT, VISIT

www.keyholefarm.com

CPSIA information can be obtained
at www.ICGtesting.com
Printed in the USA
LVHW062132250319
611825LV00012B/661/P